In 1935 if you wanted to
read a good book, you needed
either a lot of money or a library card.
Cheap paperbacks were available, but their
poor production generally mirrored the quality
between the covers. One weekend that year,
Allen Lane, Managing Director of The Bodley Head,
having spent the weekend visiting Agatha Christie,
found himself on a platform at Exeter station trying to
find something to read for his journey back to London.
He was appalled by the quality of the material he had to
choose from. Everything that Allen Lane achieved from that
day until his death in 1970 was based on a passionate belief
in the existence of 'a vast reading public for *intelligent*
books at a low price'. The result of his momentous vision
was the birth not only of Penguin, but of the 'paperback
revolution'. Quality writing became available for the price of
a packet of cigarettes, literature became a mass medium
for the first time, a nation of book-borrowers became a
nation of book-buyers – and the very concept of book
publishing was changed for ever. Those founding
principles – of quality and value, with an overarching
belief in the fundamental importance of reading –
have guided everything the company has
done since 1935. Sir Allen Lane's
pioneering spirit is still very much alive
at Penguin in 2005. Here's to
the next 70 years!

MORE THAN A BUSINESS

'We decided it was time to end the almost customary half-hearted manner in which cheap editions were produced – as though the only people who could possibly want cheap editions must belong to a lower order of intelligence. We, however, believed in the existence in this country of a vast reading public for intelligent books at a low price, and staked everything on it'
Sir Allen Lane, 1902–1970

'The Penguin Books are splendid value for sixpence, so splendid that if other publishers had any sense they would combine against them and suppress them'
George Orwell

'More than a business … a national cultural asset'
Guardian

'When you look at the whole Penguin achievement you know that it constitutes, in action, one of the more democratic successes of our recent social history'
Richard Hoggart

Nothing Bad Ever Happens in Tiffany's

MARIAN KEYES

PENGUIN BOOKS

PENGUIN BOOKS

Published by the Penguin Group
Penguin Books Ltd, 80 Strand, London WC2R ORL, England
Penguin Group (USA) Inc., 375 Hudson Street, New York, New York 10014, USA
Penguin Group (Canada), 10 Alcorn Avenue, Toronto, Ontario, Canada M4V 3B2
(a division of Pearson Penguin Canada Inc.)
Penguin Ireland, 25 St Stephen's Green, Dublin 2, Ireland
(a division of Penguin Books Ltd)
Penguin Group (Australia), 250 Camberwell Road, Camberwell, Victoria 3124,
Australia (a division of Pearson Australia Group Pty Ltd)
Penguin Books India Pvt Ltd, 11 Community Centre,
Panchsheel Park, New Delhi – 110 017, India
Penguin Group (NZ), cnr Airborne and Rosedale Roads, Albany,
Auckland 1310, New Zealand (a division of Pearson New Zealand Ltd)
Penguin Books (South Africa) (Pty) Ltd, 24 Sturdee Avenue,
Rosebank 2196, South Africa

Penguin Books Ltd, Registered Offices: 80 Strand, London WC2R ORL, England

www.penguin.com

Versions of *Cheaper than Drugs*, *Stack'n'Fly*, *36 Hours in Jo'burg*
and *Eyes Wide Shut* previously published in *Abroad* magazine
Versions of *I Shop, Therefore I Am* and *Villa-itis* previously published in *Cara* magazine
This selection first published as a Pocket Penguin 2005

I

Copyright © Marian Keyes, 2005
All rights reserved

The moral right of the author has been asserted

Set in 11/13pt Monotype Dante
Typeset by Palimpsest Book Production Limited
Polmont, Stirlingshire
Printed in England by Clays Ltd, St Ives plc

Except in the United States of America, this book is sold subject
to the condition that it shall not, by way of trade or otherwise, be lent,
re-sold, hired out, or otherwise circulated without the publisher's
prior consent in any form of binding or cover other than that in
which it is published and without a similar condition including this
condition being imposed on the subsequent purchaser

Contents

Passport Out of Here

Many years ago I was living in London and about to visit New York for the first time – my sister had moved there four months previously, and I was going to spend Christmas with her. Three nights before the off I began to pack and when I looked in my 'official things' drawer for my passport, there it was – gone! Except it couldn't be. It had sat in that drawer since I'd last needed it, on a trip to Greece the previous summer. I rummaged through bills and stuff expecting it to appear and when it didn't I took the entire contents out and systematically went through each item one by one – *nada*. My mouth went a little dry, my heart-rate increased but I told myself that it *was* here, I just couldn't see it – hadn't my mother always told me that I couldn't find the water in the river?

But unless it had become invisible, it simply Was Not There. With sweaty hands I began to tear my room apart, going through every pocket of every item of clothing in my wardrobe, looking in old rucksacks and handbags, pulling books out of my bookcase, but although I stumbled across a handful of sandy drachmas and half a bag of inexplicably abandoned Maltesers (still edible, quite nice actually), there was no passport. Then I launched an attack on the rest of the flat. Late into the night I finally had to admit the inadmissable: my passport wasn't here. At this stage I was almost whimpering with terror; although my ticket to New York had put a huge dent in my meagre finances, it was non-changeable and non-refundable. If I hadn't a passport in two days' time I wouldn't be going.

I rang my mother in Ireland. There was nothing she could do but, selfish brat that I was, a trouble shared is a trouble doubled and at least she promised to pray to Saint Anthony – for those not familiar with the superstitions of Catholicism, the idea is you pray to Saint Anthony when you lose stuff and if it turns up you make a donation to the poor box. Under normal circumstances I poured scathing scorn on the notion but right now I was so desperate that I nearly considered doing it myself.

I went to bed in my bomb-site bedroom but I barely slept and got up again at about five a.m., dervishing through the silent flat, looking behind boxes of breakfast cereals, inside video cases and when I arrived at work I was a hollow-eyed manic wreck, with the taste of panic in my mouth.

I spilled the terrible story to my boss Charlotte and she calmly advised me to apply for a new passport.

'But it takes weeks to get a passport and I leave in two days' time!' I had to try hard not to screech.

'Ring the Irish Embassy, tell them it's an emergency and send a courier for an application form.'

Within an hour, the application form was on my desk and Charlotte helped me read through the requirements because I was so frenzied the letters kept dancing in front of my eyes. First I needed a photo so she combed my hair, dispatched me to a nearby photobooth and reminded me to smile. (The photo is still in my passport, I'm a pretty shade of pistachio green.)

Next, I needed a professional to endorse my photo and my bank manager seemed the obvious choice. However, despite the lively, almost-daily correspondence that zipped from her to me, despite the audacious way she addressed me and the intimacy of her advice, she elected not to know me.

So Charlotte got on the phone and tried a magistrate she knew, but he turned out to be on holiday. Undaunted, she found a nearby barrister who owed her a favour and who was prepared to bend the rules and pretend that he knew me. I nipped round to him, then back to the office where Charlotte told me I could catch up on work later and pushed me out the door, shouting, 'Go, go, go!' like I was an SAS man parachuting into enemy territory.

Then, gasping for breath, I was running through the streets of Belgravia, counting the numbers on the wedding-cake rococo mansions, looking for the Irish Embassy. I found it and panted up the steps to the fancy front door, then back down again with a flea in my ear – the passport office was round the side and in the basement. Down the rickety spiral staircase I went, burst through the door – and suddenly I was no longer in toney Belgravia but in a sub-post-office in Athlone. It was a tiny little place, with four rows of plastic chairs cowering beneath merciless strip lighting and a serving counter with three glass hatches. I grabbed a ticket: number 792. When was my turn? I looked around for the number display and there, in hellish red digital, was the next number in line. It read 23. My heart almost leapt out of my chest with panic. I'd be here for ever! But no one was in sight, either in the waiting area or behind the counter . . .

Then from some hidden back room, a plumpish young man appeared, came up to one of the hatches, looked at me and declared, 'Next!'

I looked in confusion at my ticket.

'Next,' he repeated.

'But . . .' I flapped my little piece of paper.

'Oh, we don't bother with that yoke.'

Fair enough. Up I stepped and blurted out the tragic tale of the missing passport, the non-refundable, non-changeable ticket, the lonely sister sitting out her first Christmas in New York and he listened, leaning easily on his elbow, nodding in sympathy. 'I see, I see, I see. Do you have a couch?'

Nonplussed, I stopped in my tracks. What was going on? Was he trying to sell me furniture?

'See, you wouldn't credit the things that get lost down the back of a couch.'

'I looked down the back of the couch.'

'But did you *really* look?' he persisted. 'Did you put your hand in?' He undulated his hand in front of my face. 'Like this?'

Yes, I said. Yes, I did. And he muttered to himself,

4

'Looked down back of couch,' and appeared to tick something on a piece of paper but it was to the side of the glass and I couldn't really see it properly.

'Okay. Have you drawers?'

Excuse me?

'Desk drawers?' he elaborated. 'Some of them have a spring mechanism and you'd be amazed what gets caught in them. You really need to give them a good shake.'

I insisted that I had, although none of the drawers in my melamine chest of drawers had any kind of mechanism, but the panic was building again and threatening to choke me.

'Shook out desk drawer,' he told himself and seemed to make another tick on the piece of paper.

'Finally, have you prayed to Saint Anthony?' (As God is my witness, I'm not making any of this up.)

I admitted that I personally hadn't and he looked like he was gearing up to tell me to go away and come back after I'd had a good pray – then I played my ace. My mother was praying round the clock!

'She is, is she?' He studied me carefully.

'Round the clock,' I gasped. 'I swear.'

'Right,' he sighed. 'If Saint Anthony has been prayed to and it hasn't turned up, then it really is lost.' An arm movement that could have been the final tick on his checklist. 'We'd better organise you a new passport, so.'

Under the glass hatch I slid in my thick bundle of documentation – the application form, photos, birth cert (which bizarrely I had a copy of at my office) and photocopies of my plane tickets which Charlotte had suggested I bring in case they needed to be convinced of the urgency of my case. Your man picked up my photo. 'Not the most flattering of pictures,' he remarked. 'Mind you, they never are. Right, all of this is in order. All you have to do now is pay.'

'Here, here.' I thrust thirty quid at him (which Charlotte had lent me because all my spare cash was in traveller's cheques awaiting unloading in the Zara on 59th and Lexington).

'You pay at the Cashiers. That's the next hatch.' He slid the bundle of papers under the glass hatch and back to me, and I stepped three feet to my left to the next hatch, the one that said Cashier. At the same time he stepped three feet to his right. For a moment we eyed each other through the new glass and he said (and I'd say he was joking, I *hope* he was joking), 'Can I help you?'

Once again I slid the bundle of paper under the glass to him and this time he took the money.

'Come back tomorrow,' he said, 'and we'll have a new passport for you.'

The following day Charlotte once again gave me time off work to go to the Irish Embassy and collect the passport. When they gave me my pristine new passport I couldn't let go of it – I kept opening it and closing it and reading my name, just to make sure it was mine – and the following day I was on a plane to New York.

Cheaper than Drugs

I know a man who denies that jetlag exists. He regularly flies halfway across the world, marches off the plane after a twenty-seven hour flight, goes straight into the Auckland office, pausing only to brush his teeth, and immediately starts barking orders and making people redundant. (Or whatever super-macho, no-human-weakness job it is he does.) I want to sue this man – as far as I'm concerned denying jetlag is like denying that the earth is round. I am so prone to jetlag that I even get it when I haven't been on a plane: I get jetlag when the clocks go back. (It's because I'm so in thrall to sleep. I'm grand if I get my habitual sixteen hours a night, but if anything happens to interfere with that, I'm all over the place. I am a *martyr* to my circadian rhythms.)

Naturally, I've investigated all the jetlag 'cures': stay away from the jar on the plane; drink plenty of water; eat lightly; do a little exercise; get on to local time patterns immediately; and, most importantly, walk around in the sunlight as soon as you arrive at your faraway destination.

All nonsense, of course: as effective as giving someone a Barbie plaster for a shattered femur. I must admit I don't trust 'natural' solutions to conditions – I like chemicals. I am probably the last person in the Western World who doesn't have a homeopath and who still swears by antibiotics. I would *love* it if someone invented an anti-jetlag drug and I couldn't care less about side-effects, in fact I'd embrace them. Dry mouth? Trembling? Blurred vision? Better than being fecking jetlagged and falling asleep face-downwards in my dinner at six in the evening. But, unfortunately, for some things there is no cure but time. Like a hangover or a broken heart, you just have to wait your jetlag out and try to live through it as best you can.

Of all the suggested 'cures' I think that trying to get on to local time as quickly as possible is probably the best, but doing it is so phenomenally unpleasant. Walking around on feet I can no longer feel, swimming through air that seems lit with little silvery tadpoles, the pavement lurching towards me – everything takes on a strange, hallucinogenic quality. (Mind you, if you're that way inclined, it'll save you a fortune in recreational drugs.)

In Australia, I had the worst ever example of this. In a pitiful attempt to recover from a twenty-four hour flight and an eleven hour time difference, myself and Himself thought we'd 'do a little exercise' and 'walk around in the sunlight' as soon as we arrived. It was early evening and, clutching our bottles of water, ('drink plenty of water') we staggered about on an area of greenness so verdant that we gradually realised it must be a golf-course. Bumping into each other and grumpily apologising, like we were scuttered, I suddenly saw

8

something that stopped me so abruptly in my tracks it was like I'd run into an invisible wall. Through the gathering gloom, about twenty feet away, were two kangaroos who were kicking the CRAP out of each other. Balancing on their tail and laying into their sparring partner with powerful 'whump's, I could actually *feel* the impacts. They were kicking each other so hard and fast it was like they were doing kung fu.

It was then that I got a bad dose of The Fear. 'Please tell me,' I clutched Himself's arm, 'please tell me that you see them too.' (He said, 'See what?' but he was only messing, thank Christ.)

However, jetlag isn't all bad. It's a great excuse to go out and get pure stotious, on the principle that if you're sick and psychotic with a hangover, you won't notice the jetlag. Or if you were planning a nervous breakdown, now's your chance. You'll be feeling alienated and fearful anyway, you might as well double up. And my own personal favourite – jetlag affords the perfect opportunity to eat guilt-free Toblerones at two in the morning. Picture it – it's pitch-black outside, a deep blanket of sleep has settled on whatever strange city you're in, and suddenly, as if you've just been plugged into the mains, you're AWAKE. You're super-awake, you've never before been this alert in your *life*. You're so firing on all cylinders that you could go on *Who Wants to be a Millionaire?* and win it in fifteen minutes. And you're also hungry. Savagely so. Your poor stomach is still on home time; it had to miss its breakfast and it's not best pleased that someone wants to deprive it of its lunch as well. But deep in the bowels of the silent, sleeping hotel, the room service lads have shut up shop and gone home and it's a long, long wait until morning.

What choice have you but to shine the luminous light of the mini-bar into the darkened room and select an over-priced, super-sized bag of M&Ms and clamber back into bed to eat yourself back to sleep?

See? Not all bad.

Stack'n'Fly

'It is better to travel than to arrive.'

Whoever said that should get his head examined. It is NOT better to travel. To travel is AWFUL and to arrive is LOVELY.

The only time it's not entirely unbearable to travel is when you're on the Orient Express, and your daily champagne allowance would fell an elephant. Or on a cruise liner the size of a small country, and you're sailing from place to place but it doesn't feel like it, the same way you don't feel the earth turning at four million miles a day (or whatever it is.)

Let's look at how awful it is to TRAVEL, will we? I won't even mention the car-clogged crawl to the airport, the dog-eat-dog scramble for parking and the overland trek from the long-stay car park to the departures hall. (All I'll say is that I've heard frequent travellers discussing the feasibility of paying homeless people to sleep in a space in the short-term A car park, so that it'll be reserved for them for when they need it.)

Anyway . . . Having arrived at Departures but already lost the will to live, I look up at the telly monitors wondering where I should check in. But I needn't bother over-exerting my neck muscles by looking *up*. All I need to do is look *in*, at the rowdy, pushing, shoving mass of humanity spilling out into the set-down area. It might look like a riot at a Red Cross feeding station but actually it's a queue. A queue filled with shrieking babies all sporting ear-infections, over-excited teenage boys playfully breaking each others limbs and greasy long-haired men wanting to check-in rocket launchers and garden sheds. Step right this way, Miss Keyes!

For many, many hours I shuffle, far too slowly for any movement to be visible to the naked eye, and because – through no fault of my own – I'm one of the last to check in, all the good seats are gone. I'm usually told it's not possible for the left side and right side of my body to sit together, so one half of me will sit in 11B and the other in 23E.

I then proceed to Security in order to be groped and to display the contents of my brain on a little table. (Okay, security checks are a very good thing, I'm just sore because recently I was relieved of some of my finest tweezers in a handbag search. Very expensive they were too, something people don't seem to realise about tweezers. They think they only cost a couple of euro, but mine cost *eighteen quid*. Sterling.) The security check eventually comes to an end and when I've replaced my internal organs in something approximating to their correct configuration, I proceed to the gate – just in time for the delay!

Now the thing is, I expect delays, I don't even mind them (apart from when I miss my connecting flight to Mauritius). I've learnt to embrace them in a Zen kind of way – why resent them? Resenting them would be as futile as resenting the sun rising in the morning. Delays *are*.

What I mind are the delay-related lies, the massive conspiracy that every airport employee is in on – the 'Delay? What Delay?' fiction. Sometimes I try to con the check-in person by asking, all super-innocent, 'How long is the delay?' And just before they yawn and say, 'Oh, you know, the usual, about an hour and ten,' they suddenly flick me a furtive, fearful glance and go, '*Delay*? What delay?' We're treated just like small children on a long car journey who ask their mammy, 'Are we there yet?'. Instead of the mammy saying brusquely, 'It's another three hours, so just get fecking-well used to it,' she fobs them off with, 'Soon, love, soon.' However, I would rather know the facts, unpalatable as they might be, because then I could quite happily go round the shops and try out lipsticks on the back of my hand, instead of sitting anxiously at the gate watching the greasy long-haired men polishing their rocket launchers. But when I've pleaded, 'Just tell me the truth,' the response has been, 'The truth?' Mad B-movie cackle. 'You can't HANDLE the truth.'

But no night is too long and finally, on we get! Most planes smell a bit funny now because the airlines have 'cut back on' (euphemism for abolished) their cleaning staff, but who's complaining? God Almighty, when did a bad smell ever kill anyone? We can spray perfume on hankies and keep them clamped to our faces; it worked fine in Elizabethan times, why not now?

Anyway, so I take my seat and calmly wait to be joined by the twenty-stone person with personal hygiene issues who is invariably seated next to me. But once in a blue moon the unthinkable happens and the seat beside me remains empty. Other passengers flood in and sit down and still no one gets in beside me. I hardly dare let myself hope. Like, what are the chances? *No I won't let myself think it, I won't even entertain the thought.* But then the trolley dollies start making their 'Cross-check' and 'Cross-hatch' noises and my hope can no longer be contained. It breaks free and goes on the rampage. Could it possibly be . . . ? Have I really been given the luxury of space and privacy and fragrant-ish air for this flight? Thank you God, oh thank you!

And then I hear it: the faint pounding noise, which gets nearer and louder. Please God, no, I beg. I can actually feel it now, the plane is slightly shaking with each rumble – the unmistakable sound of a twenty-stone smelly person running down the walk-way. With a sinking heart I hear the groan of metal straining as he steps onto the plane and makes his way directly towards me, the floor buckling and creaking with each step. After ten minutes banging and clattering, as he tries to fit his rocket launcher into the overhead compartment, he fights his way into his seat, gives me a gap-toothed smile and unwraps his kebab.

If only that was all I had to endure, but as airlines have also cut back on (i.e. abolished) their maintenance staff, I usually spend the flight with my table tray crashing down onto my knees every time the person in the seat in front breathes.

Eventually we reach our destination, and after we have staved off the curse of Icarus and prevented the wings from falling off, by completing the ritual thirty circles over the entire city, we're allowed to land. Only to discover – why, why, why? – we have to sit on the tarmac like a crowd of goms because they can't find a set of steps for us. This is the point where I start talking to myself, pretending to be the local air-traffic control people. 'A plane, you say? Landed? What, *here*? And you all want to get off? Steps, is it? And a coach? And what magic wand do you expect us to wave? Look, we'll do our best to accommodate you this once but bear in mind this is an *airport*, we're not equipped for this sort of thing.'

A speedy couple of hours polishes off the passport control, the luggage carousel, the unattended luggage desk to report the unarrived luggage and the taxi queue 'managed' by some power-crazed weirdo who understands the laws of the universe in an entirely different way to the rest of us. Then, after a soupçon of heavy traffic – finally, I ARRIVE!

Come in, they say, sit down, no, *lie* down, on a silken feather bed and have some nectar. Ambrosia, so? Chunky Kit-Kat? Wide-screen TV? Jo Malone candles? Foot-rub? Spot of reiki? Sex with George Clooney? Just say it and you can have it.

See, TRAVEL = horrible and ARRIVE = lovely.

Surely we're all agreed on it? Apparently something like 112 per cent of regular travellers say that the one thing that would transform their quality of life would be a 'Beam me up, Scotty,' machine so that they could just arrive directly at their destination and cut out all that nasty pesky travelling.

But in the absence of that, ladies and gentlemen,

let me introduce the unique Stack'n'Fly System (currently pending patent). The brainchild of seasoned traveller . . . er . . . me and my friend Malcolm – this is how it works. You check your bags in as usual, go to your gate, lie down on a stretcher, get strapped in, then a nurse comes along and administers a knock-out shot. You're totally out cold and until you arrive at your destination, you know nothing. Not delays, not kebab-man, nothing. The seats would be removed from the planes so that several stretchers could be stacked on top of each other, not unlike the onboard catering trollies (which, of course, there would no longer be any need for). That way there would be room for the airlines to get loads more passengers in, so everyone's happy.

Instead of air-hostesses on board, we'd have a nurse who'd patrol the aisle with a hypodermic syringe, just in case someone starts to come to, too early. Fantastic, eh? And that's just how it would work in Economy. Business Class passengers would be guaranteed a deluxe service where an ambulance-style vehicle would come to their home and give them their injection right there, so they'd be spared *everything* – the drive, the check-in, the groping, the delays. Same at the other end – still unconscious, a whole stack of them and their clicky pens could be wheeled through passport control, baggage etc. and they need know nothing until they'd ARRIVED and everyone's running around being lovely to them.

I have seen the future and it's sedated.

36 Hours in Jo'burg

A few years ago I went on a book-tour of South Africa. It was
the beginning of my love affair with this magical continent.
Before the work started, I had a day and a half in Johannesburg.

The thing is, Johannesburg has a terrible reputation for
violence and certainly, on the drive from the airport,
all the houses looked like grim, blank-faced fortresses.
So my publishers had installed Himself and myself in
a cosy hotel in a safe suburb where we were less likely
to get raped and shot. However, I'd been all geared up
for African 'otherness' and almost cried at our red,
swirly carpet and pink, flowery room. It looked like
Surrey.

Disconsolate, I switched on the telly looking for the
South African *Who Wants to be a Millionaire?* (I was keen
to add to my collection, I'd seen it in Japanese, Czech
and German) and instead I found the pan-African news
and I was shot through with a deep thrill at being on
this vast continent.

Because we'd come in on an overnight flight, we slept
for a lot of the day, which was lucky because we were
under the strictest instruction to go nowhere on our
own. *Nowhere.*

Around seven that evening, just as the rose-covered walls were starting to close in, Karen, my publicity girl, sprung us and took us to an area full of bars, restaurants, music and throngs of tall, thin Xhosa and Zulu. Not a bit like Surrey. I cheered up a bit. But after Karen had parked her jeep, she foraged for a rand, to give to the guys minding the cars. She muttered something about how embarrassing all this need for security was, so I told her how we have the same situation in Ireland, how they're called lock-hard men . . . then I noticed something and abruptly, I shut up. Irish lock-hard men don't carry AK-47s.

On Sunday morning I had a hair appointment. (And as the salon was actually *in* the hotel Karen was prepared to let me go without an escort.) Now, a quick word about my hair. It's thick, frizzy and unruly and only a highly skilled professional can tame it. I had a week of publicity ahead of me, kicking off with South Africa's version of *Ireland AM* very early the following morning – too early to get my hair done before it – so Karen had arranged that the hotel's hairdresser come in specially.

He was a prissy Swiss bloke and very narky about having to work on a Sunday. But he was one of those passive-aggressive types who told me he didn't mind, it's just that Sunday is his only day off, and that if he doesn't get enough rest, he gets ill, he had a really bad throat infection last month, he's prone to throat infections when he doesn't get enough rest, but don't get him wrong, he doesn't *mind*. So when he 'showed' me a phial of special expensive gear which mends split-ends (as if!) and told me I was under no obligation to buy it, I felt obliged to buy it.

When I returned to the room, Himself leapt to his feet and, in ragged tones, told me the rose-covered walls were moving in on him again. However Karen had told us that if we wanted to go out, to call her. But I didn't want to bother her on a Sunday. (She might make me buy more stuff for my split-ends.)

A dilemma ensued. From our window we could see a shopping centre only fifty yards up the road; it didn't look like the sort of place you'd get raped and shot. But then I thought of the men with the AK-47s – and they were the good guys.

In the end we decided to chance it but, on the short walk, I felt as if I was in Sarajevo, in danger of being picked off by sniper fire. The gas thing was the place looked like Donaghmede shopping centre, all small and ordinary, but there was a market on, jammers with African carvings and metalwork, bizarre-looking vegetables and smells of exotic cooking. It was intense, exciting and crammed with Bantu, Indians, even one or two whites. *Nothing* like Donaghmede. Or Sarajevo.

Everyone was lovely, no one tried to kill us and I bought an embroidered tablecloth – what was to become the inaugural tablecloth in my Tablecloths-bought-on-booktours collection. (Funny thing is, I'm not a tablecloth kind of person. Must have been the stress.) We even had our lunch before returning to the hotel.

Giddy and elated with having cheated death, we got through a good portion of the afternoon before the walls began to close in again. We had to get out. Earlier we'd noticed a small cinema in the shopping centre and after so successfully avoiding being murdered on our previous outing, we decided to give it a whirl. All that was on was *Chocolat* and under normal circumstances we might have made fun of its tweeness, but in our fragile, dislocated states, it was exactly what we needed. However, when we emerged from the cinema, it had started to rain. As an Irish woman, I thought I knew all there was to know about rain. But this African stuff took it to the next level: water tumbled from the sky and ricocheted off the pavements in great bucketloads.

Himself said, 'We'll be drenched.'

Drenched? We'd be concussed. And worse again, if I went out in that deluge, the narky Swiss man's work would be entirely undone in two seconds and I'd have to go on telly the following morning looking like Jack Osborne. We waited ten anxious minutes; it got noticeably worse. The roads had become fast-flowing torrents and not a car was about. Back in, looking for something to protect my hair. The only shop still open was the pick'n'mix and I explained my situation to the lovely Xhosa woman. From a sheet of cellophane, she fashioned a cunning rain-hat, like a hanky knotted at four corners that English men used to wear on the beach. (The cleaning staff had got wind that a human drama was unfolding in the Sweet Factory and had gathered to snigger.) Once my head was water-tight, I draped my denim jacket over it and tied the sleeves under my chin. I looked gorgeous. Not.

We could have white-water rafted home. So much rain was wrung out of our clothes, you'd swear they'd just been washed. But my hair? Well, my hair was perfect.

Being Sent to Siberia

News arrived! I was being sent to Russia! To some place called Novosibirsk. I was extremely pleased as I'd always wanted to visit somewhere ending in 'sk'. I'd favoured Omsk, Tomsk and Murmansk, but Novosibirsk would do nicely.

But where in the vastness of Russia *was* Novosibirsk? 'We'll buy the city guide to it.'

Oh, how we laughed. The laughing stopped, however, when I looked it up on the internet. Himself had left the room and I nearly shouted the house down for him to come and have a look. 'Himself! HIMSELF! I've found out where it is. Novosibirsk is the capital of SiBEEEERia.'

He nearly broke his neck running and in grim silence we stood before the screen and scrolled down through the details. Average temperature in February (which was when we were going) -16°C. Dropping as low as -35°C. 'We'll need gloves,' we concluded. Then trying to establish the time difference was tricky. Eight hours ahead of GMT. 'Unless they have daylight saving time?' 'D'you think they have any daylight to save?' I countered bitterly.

In the following weeks we wrung much hollow laughter from the situation by telling people at every opportunity that we were being sent to Siberia.

How to keep warm became all we talked about. We

shopped for thermal underwear – quartering the average age as soon as we walked into the super-warm-knickers emporium – and passionately we debated the rights and wrongs of fur coats, a debate abruptly abandoned once we discovered how much fur coats actually cost. Then word came – a change of plans! We weren't going to Siberia after all! Other parts of Russia instead, all quite cold too, just not as cold as Siberia. We were mortified as, by then, we were dining out nightly on our gulag story. Our credibility was in shreds.

Day one

Wearing an awful lot of clothes, we landed in Moscow. At Immigration, I was quite annoyed at how quickly they processed us. Call itself Russia! I wanted to queue, I wanted the authentic experience.

Outside in the perishing cold with sleet in the air and dirty slush underfoot, we met Valya, who would be our guide/minder for the trip. She was fresh-faced and blue-eyed, with blonde hair swirled like two danish pastries over her ears. As soon as we'd said hello, she told us that her husband had just left her. God, I love Russians. *Love* them. They'll tell you *anything*. They do unhappiness with such verve, such style, such passion. As we lugged our suitcase to the car, Valya told me that she had nothing left to live for, but that she would still take care of us on the tour.

We had a driver, Boris, to take us into the centre of

Moscow and he looked so unhappy it was almost comical. He had a wide, clown mouth that turned down at the corners. His girl had just left him, Valya told us. After a short conversation in Russian, she divulged it had been for a younger man. Another burst of chat. Who happened to be his brother. I sensed a matchmaking moment coming on. 'You wouldn't consider your man, as a replacement for your husband?' I asked her.

She considered Boris, then curled her lip. 'He is not good at making the sex.'

'But how do you know?'

'It is why his girl left him. He drinks too much. He wets the bed.'

Ah, well . . .

We only had four hours in Moscow before catching the overnight train east, just enough time to see there was a Chanel shop in Red Square (Lenin must be rotating in his grave like a great big oul kebab) and to be stopped twice by military police looking for our papers. Everyone always says how grey and grim Russia is, but in Red Square is Saint Basil's Cathedral, the most beautiful building I've ever seen. It's what someone might dream up on a good acid trip: turrets and spires and onion domes, swirled like ice-cream cones, all decked out in magnificent carnival colours. Commissioned by Ivan the Terrible, he was so pleased with it that he poked out the architect's eyes. (So he couldn't ever do a cathedral for anyone else – a real mark of respect, your man must've been thrilled.)

Over dinner, in a smoke-filled wannabe-brasserie, Valya

tried to make herself heard over the ear-blistering techno, to tell us more about her husband doing a runner.

'Maybe he'll come back,' I bellowed hopefully.

'He will not.' She said it matter-of-factly, doing that lovely Russian honest/pessimistic thing. Valya was fabulous. (And just a small bit mad, as befits a woman who has just been left by her husband.) I loved her. I am always at my happiest with slightly mad people.

Then it was time to get the train. Moscow station was like a vision of hell: desperate-looking, unshaven men standing about in the perishing cold, looking for an unofficial portering gig. Everywhere were little kiosks selling drink, they were doing a brisk trade.

To my surprise, the train came on time *and* it was gorgeous. Our sleeper carriage was like a cottage on wheels, with two little beds, old-fashioned, patterned blankets and chintz curtains at the windows. Wood-panelling lined the walls and it was all cosy and lovely. Just as soon as they turned off the deafening techno.

We rattled though the snowy night, between two short points on this enormous landmass.

Day two

By morning we had arrived in the beautiful city of Nizhny Novgorod. (I love saying that. 'I was in Nizzz-hhhhhny Novgorod, you know.' Even now, I still look for chances – however tenuous – to drop it into conversations. 'So you like chocolate, do you? Funnily enough,

I had some lovely chocolate in Nizzzhhhny Novgorod.')

God it was cold, though, the kind of cold where it hurts to breathe. Although not by local standards – they were having a heat-wave. Normally, at that time of year, it was thirty below, but this was a balmy, unseasonable minus ten.

We were met by a wonderful young man called Artim and checked into our hotel, the dinkiest, cosiest, most charming place. From our bedroom window we could see children ice-skating on a frozen football pitch. I felt very far from home. In a nice way.

My first gig was a creative-writing session with some university students. Artim, Valya, Himself and I descended into the bowels of a violet-walled nightclub, where said students slumped around, reassuringly surly and disenchanted. I beamed with pleasure. I can't be doing with those eager, puppy-eyed teenagers who are keen to learn. It's not natural.

My next engagement was a television interview. Off we all went in Artim's car, our numbers swelled further by a sweet, if slightly smelly, student called Pyotr who'd developed a crush on me in the violet-walled nightclub. We were stopped twice by military police en route to the telly station.

The interviewer was a skinny, super-intense bloke who called himself Ed and who wanted to talk about 'art'.

'Would you die for your art?'

Well, of course I wouldn't. But I didn't want to disappoint him, so I nodded yes, certainly, indeed'n I would.

But then he threw a curve ball. 'We have just heard the tragic news that your Princess Margaret has died. Would you like to say something?'

Caught on the hop, I said the first thing that came into my head. 'They should have let her marry the man she loved. The bastards.'

This caused confusion. 'You do not love your royal family?'

'Irish, see? Not mine.'

More confusion. When the interview ended, we decided to go for a drink and Ed said he'd come too. And so would his researcher. By now, my entourage had swelled to Jennifer Lopez-size proportions.

Back in the hotel, before we went out for dinner, myself and Himself were hit by a sudden longing for coffee. Luckily we had sachets – they'd been in our little welcome packs on the train – all we needed was boiling water, so I volunteered to try out my Russian on the hotel staff. Standing in front of the mirror, I practiced a few times: a gracious smile, then *'Zdrastvuti.'* (Hello.)' *'Voda, pazhalsta.'* (Water, please.) Down I went, smiled at the lady and delivered the line.

'Hmmm?' she went. 'Oh! You want hot water? Would you like it here or in your room? Whichever you like, it's up to you.'

'Er, right. Up in the room so.'

(Helpful hint for you here, which I discovered entirely by accident because I wanted to cool my coffee down so I could drink it: if you want a cappucino but you don't have access to a machine, you could try adding carbonated Russian water to your coffee. It fizzes and froths like something in a scientific experiment. Funnily enough, it doesn't seem to work with non-Russian water.)

Then we went out for dinner and were stopped about sixteen times by the military police on the way to the restaurant. I was starting to recognise some of them. We had a lovely evening, the people were so intelligent, warm and funny, tinging even their saddest stories with a very attractive irony. I LOVE Russians. I want to be one. The thing about them is, in an increasingly homogenous world, they're so *Russian*. And when the bill came, the Russians flung themselves at it, doing that thing that Irish people do, wrestling people to the ground, trying to pay for everything. See, I like that.

Day three

I met Valya on the way down for breakfast and made the mistake of asking, 'How did you sleep?'

Most people would just say, 'Fine.' But Valya rendered a blow-by-blow account of her feelings. Clopping down the stairs to the breakfast room, she said, 'I am thinking about him making the sex with his new one and I cannot sleep. I smoke all night and think of him making the sex with me instead.'

Still talking loudly about making the sex, we entered a neat little dining room with white linen embroidered tablecloths and napkins. Everything was charmingly twee, apart from the telly blasting out techno at a level that felt like a physical assault, and the fug of cigarette smoke obscuring the sideboard of food.

That afternoon we proceeded to the town hall – Nizhny Novgorod was having an arts festival and I was the star exhibit! The place was jammers, the atmosphere was bouyant and lovely people kept appearing to practise their English on me, except Pyotr kept trying to shoo them away so he could have me to his (smelly) self. Then it was showtime and just as I mounted the stage to start my reading, the lights flickered, once, twice, then disappeared entirely. What the . . . ? It was the electricity! We were having a power cut. A lovely, authentic Russian power cut! Was it the real thing or were they just laying it on for us tourists?

Oh, it seemed to be the real thing, all right. Everyone was rushing around and people kept promising me, 'This never happens. *Never!*'

Enquiries were made: was it a localised thing? Just the nightclub, perhaps? But no, the whole town was out. Even though it was only three in the afternoon, it was quite dark. A decision was made: I would do my reading by candlelight. But I couldn't read and hold my candle at the same time, in case I set my book on fire, so the love-struck Pyotr was on his feet, offering to hold my candle. As it were. So the show went on, with Pyotr taking every opportunity to stand far too close to me. But hey, I was facing forty and flattered.

Afterwards, I fell among poets. There was a load of them in the front row, several looking like James Joyce, right down to the flattened hair, roundy glasses and sober suits. They grabbed me as I stepped off the stage and all gave me signed copies of their slender volumes. Although I couldn't understand a word they were saying, they were a right laugh.

Armed with home-printed books of Russian poetry, I returned to Valya and Himself and we watched a little drama in mime. (It ended tragically.) Then someone sang a song. (A sad one.) Then there was a stand-up comedian. (A special, unfunny Russian one.)

But then there was some sort of disturbance. A kerfuffle. The poets seemed to be staging some kind of anarchic takeover. There were an awful lot of them, crowding onto the small stage, looking like Kool and the Gang. Then a guitar appeared and they wouldn't stop singing.

It was a great, *great* afternoon – everyone had been so nice. But Artim, the wonderful man who had organised it all, wouldn't take the praise. 'It's those damn poets,' he said. 'They stage a takeover every year and this year they *promised*.'

Day four

Up horribly, horribly early to catch the plane to Samara – too early even for the techno, smoke-filled breakfast.

The week before I'd been in the US and got mightily humbled for having tweezers in my hand-luggage, so Himself made me promise that I had nothing dangerous on my person for this flight. Not that it mattered a damn. I could have carried a ground-to-air rocket launcher onto the plane and no one would have minded. They'd probably have helped me lift it on.

It was a novel flying experience. Nothing was screened through any metal detector yokes and the plane itself looked like a toy, with steps that went up from under into its belly. There were no conveyor belts or chance to check in luggage: you had to carry on all your own stuff – suitcases, rocket launchers, etc. Then, when I first emerged up into the body of the aircraft, I thought it was one of those military planes with no seats, where you sit on the metal floor waiting to parachute out over enemy territory. But, mercifully, behind a little curtain there were seats. Sort of. There were chintz curtains on the windows and no working seatbelts. Everyone was frozen, you could see the cold air when you breathed out and they all kept their furry hats on. It was like being on a rattley old bus going between Knock and Claremorris on a wet January day. Think about that the next time you're tempted to complain about Ryanair.

And the thing was, I knew that this was the safest airline in Russia.

Nothing to eat, mind you. *Nothing to eat*. And now it was getting to me.

Between the hunger and the tiredness and the strangeness of everything and being in the grip of mad, bad PMS, I behaved very badly in Samara. I was in a right fouler and I just couldn't bury it. (I'm still so ashamed of myself.

It's one of those memories that, whenever it surfaces, makes me wish I was dead. You know those ones? Even writing about it is killing me, but it must be done.)

When we landed, our lovely driver took us on a tour of Samara. Until very recently it was a closed city. (They used to make bomber planes and other secret stuff.) It was a big banana to be allowed to visit and, in all fairness, it was beautiful and the Volga was frozen over and men were sitting fishing into little holes in the ice and it was all very atmospheric and charming, but I couldn't care less. I wanted something to eat.

Instead I had to do a press conference.

After which we were finally let eat something. Our host led us along a slushy, pot-holed street, to a pancake place, where he ushered us to the cloakroom and said, 'Here. Please to take your clothes off.' And I was too narky to even raise a smile.

Food usually does the trick with me but even after I'd eaten about fifty-six pancakes with a variety of fillings, my mood remained sour. And remained so when we arrived at the local university, where I was to adjudicate a debate. In honour of me being a recovering jarhead, the title of the debate was: *Should drugs be legalised?* It was the most one-sided debate I'd ever come across. It was clear that all the students were horrified by drugs and it kind of annoyed me, what with Russia being rife with alcoholism; why worry about keeping pot criminalised when alcohol was perfectly legal and in the process of killing and destroying more Russian lives than every other drug put together?

Anyway, I should have kept my mouth shut and smiled politely, but to my great shame I couldn't. Brutally and rudely I laid down my views and although they gave me a box of chocolates when I left, I could tell that they were thinking of keeping them for themselves. Not that I blame them. Oh the shame! The rudeness of me!

And so, finally, to our hotel, a flimsy unreassuring place which seemed to have been bought in its entirety from IKEA. (This is not a good thing, some of the unhappiest moments of my life have been spent in IKEA.)

I was feeling too ashamed to go out for dinner that night, but Valya made me. In the restaurant she was in a strangely restless mood, drinking vodka shots and on the prowl. She still loved her husband but she wouldn't mind making the sex with someone else. Your man over there, in fact, she said, pointing to a bull-necked but otherwise quite attractive man, who had surprisingly nice shoes for a Russian. I was thrilled. I'd taken violently agin the deserting husband and I wanted her to hook up with someone new. Myself and Himself wished her well, left her to it and went back to our flat-pack hotel. Some unknown time that night we were woken by an almighty crash. It sounded like a ceiling had fallen in. We'd just drifted back to sleep when we heard another. Then one more, this time so bad that Himself's wash-bag fell off the bathroom shelf. It was Valya-related, I just *knew* it.

Great excitement next morning at breakfast, when through the haze of cigarette smoke, we saw, bobbing his head along to the techno, Valya's fella from the night before. She shoots, she scores!

Unfortunately not, as it transpired that he was just another guest in the hotel. Feck! Then Valya appeared, telling the entire room, first in English, then in Russian, that she had been so drunk the night before that she had fallen into her wardrobe. (The first crash we'd heard.) Then she told everyone that she had missed her husband so much that she had rolled around with a pillow so violently that she had fallen out of bed. (The second crash.) Twice. (The third, washbag-dislocating one.)

Day five

Flight to St Petersburg. The plane was disappointingly normal. Seatbelts and the like. I much preferred the other one.

Now, St Petersburg, with its wide 'European-style' boulevards and impressively bombastic buildings, is the Russian city that everyone gets their knickers in a twist about. And yes, it's undeniably impressive and beautiful, but actually I think I preferred the smaller, more 'Russian' towns, the ones that you mightn't normally see. My work consisted of holding two workshops where I met students of English so staggeringly talented, they put me to shame.

Then it was my last afternoon, where I stumbled across – and I'm not joking here – one of the most beautiful shoe shops I've EVER been in. And let's face it, I've seen the inside of a few.

God, I love Russia.

PS Soon afterwards Valya met another bloke. He is excellent at making the sex.

PPS A few months after my return I was in County Mayo when I realised the next town I was about to drive through was called Tulsk. Tul*sk*. See my point? It ends in 'sk'. So there's no need for me to go to Murmansk, Tomsk, Omsk, Bryansk, Gdansk or Novosibirsk. But I might anyway.

I Shop, Therefore I Am

If you like to shop there is nowhere in the world like New York. You can get everything in the whole world there. Here are some highlights from a recent trip.

First stop: Saks of Fifth Avenue

We had to run the gauntlet of the cosmetics hall before getting to the lifts at the back. Himself took a nervous look at the over-fragrant melée – at the marauding gangs of sharp-suited types, lying in wait with bottles of Nu, ready to spray us, at the white-coated skin therapists, ready to ambush us with their special offers – and looked terrified.

'Just put your head down and run,' I said. 'And whatever you do, don't make eye-contact with any of them.'

I launched myself into the fray, Himself on my heels. 'Stay low, stay low!' I urged, but the inevitable happened. 'Christ! I got got,' he yelped.

'How bad?' I asked.

He sniffed himself. 'Paul Smith for women. Not too bad.'

We kept going, while all around us voices babbled a cacophany of temptations. *Hey gorgeous, wanna try our* *new Spring shades? Over here, over here, spend $75 and get a free lipstick. Never mind them, what about us, our dinky travel kits are just in. But we're showcasing our new concealer, it'll change your LIFE . . .*

Finally we reached the lifts at the back. 'Jesus,' he said, wiping the sweat from his brow. 'It's like a Moroccan souk.'

How I got barred from Miu Miu

There are many posh shops in New York and the staff are not pleasant. At least not to me. I was given some advice by a regular: Look evil and bored. Waft. Display no positive emotion. Above all, don't make a fool of yourself.

With Himself, my sister and my friend Anne-Marie in tow, we entered Miu Miu, where the first thing I saw was my favourite pair of boots – I was actually wearing a pair – at half-price. Caught up in a fifty-percent-off frenzy, I decided to buy a new pair but first I had to check the size of the ones I was wearing. So I straightened my leg and stuck my foot up for Himself to see what it said on my sole. As he held my ankle at face height (he's tall) I felt myself losing my balance and began that hopping, arm-windmilling thing people do – usually just before someone off stage throws in a bag of ball-bearings. My sister grabbed hold of me, but unfortunately also fell victim to the waves of unbalance, then Anne-Marie tried to re-verticalise us, but she too got caught up in the vortex. We hovered between balance and falling for a few tortuous seconds. Then Himself intervened but the combined weight of the three of us was too much and, in slow motion, in a tangle of limbs and coats and handbags, all four of us toppled to the floor. *Oh my God, I'm lying on the floor in Miu Miu.*

Himself refuses to go into Victoria's Secret

Just point blank refused. He didn't even say, 'Please don't make me.' He just stood at the door, looked at the prairies of underwear within, told me no power on earth would make him go in and that was that. I told him he'd look more like a pervert hanging around outside, but nothing doing.

I was keen to see what all the fuss was about; in the ads I'd got the impression that Victoria's Secret was a class act but when I stood too close to one of the night-dresses and it crackled and stuck to me, I wasn't so sure. All the same, I bought a couple of bras – one pink, one lilac. Later, when I told my sister about the visit, she said in disgust, 'Oh my God. You didn't buy anything, did you?' I fessed up the coloured bras. 'Well,' she advised, 'just don't stand in front of any naked flames.'

The psychic assistants in Bloomingdales

Anne-Marie told me the assistants in Bloomingdales were psychic and I thought she meant that they were so knowledgeable they were *almost* psychic. So myself and Himself went into Bloomingdales looking for the Eileen Fisher range and – not expecting any joy – asked an assistant if they stocked it. Without missing a beat he not only confirmed that they carried it, but gave me the exact co-ordinates (third floor, two thirds of the way back, bordered by Marc Jacobs to the north, Aqua to the east and DKNY to the south). Bearing in mind that Bloomingdales is the size of a small country I thought he was having a little joke at our expense, but went to the third floor anyway. When we got off the escalator, we stood for a nonplussed second, trying to find our bearings. 'Where . . . ?' I asked but got no further because a young man, about fifteen feet away from us called, 'Go right for twenty-two feet, then at Aqua go left and you'll find Eileen Fisher on the third island.' I stared at him nervously. 'Go on,' he urged. Uncertainly, with much looking back over our shoulders at him, we followed his instructions and found that the stand was exactly where he'd said it would be. But how had he known what we were looking for? Walkie-talkies was the only thing I could come up with; perhaps the man downstairs had radioed up and told him to expect us? Or maybe Bloomingdales just send their assistants on courses to develop their psychic skills.

Being laughed at by the Clinique girl

I approached the altar of cosmetics – tier after tier of silver-cylindered loveliness – and explained my mission. I wanted brow highlighter. My sister had some, I'd admired it, she'd got it from Clinique. But the glossy-faced girl knew of no such thing and I told her I thought it was called Sugar Sugar. 'Oh! Sugar Sugar!' she said. 'Oh yeah, I remember that.' Momentarily, she was over-come with silent, shuddery mirth. 'That's a trend item.'

'What does that mean?'

'It is so, like, OVER.'

The scary woman in Prada

I love Prada. Not so much the clothes, which are for malnourished thirteen-year-olds, but I covet, with covety covetousness, the shoes and handbags. Like, I LOVE them. If I was given a choice between world peace and a Prada handbag, I'd dither. (I am not proud of this. I'm only saying.)

Anyway, in myself and Himself go to the limestone palace on Fifth Avenue and up to the second floor to look at the accessories. I want to fling myself on the floor and sob at their beauty, but Himself reminds me of the Miu Miu debacle and I manage to contain myself.

Then I saw it. The handbag. *The* handbag. THE handbag.

Reader, I bought it. A Russian woman called Elena was my assistant and I think it must have been the quickest bit of commission she'd ever earned. Then I was kind of getting the hang of things and decided to see about matching sandals. But they didn't have them in my size. Undaunted, Elena brought them anyway. It was no go, so she brought sandals that nearly matched, then sandals that didn't match at all. And didn't fit either. But she could not be faulted for leaving a stone unturned and, reluctantly, she let me go only when it was clear that I really wasn't going to buy anything else from her.

Downstairs I'd stopped to idly admire some luggage when Elena suddenly popped up again, two inches from my nose. Somehow she'd managed to insinuate herself between me and the holdall. 'You would like to buy?'

I told her no thanks, that we really were leaving, but then we noticed that there was a menswear department in the basement. Down we went, Himself picked up a shoe and a handsome young man approached and asked if he'd like it in his size. I had just opened my mouth to reply (Himself is too scared to speak in these places) when, out-of-nowhere, Elena appeared, did a ten-yard skid across the floor of Menswear, shoved the good-looking man to the margins with her palm over his face and arrived in front of us wearing a shark's smile, not a hair out of place. 'You would like to try?'

Nothing bad ever happens in Tiffany's

Oh, Holly Golightly, how could you! You try telling that to my credit card. See, what happened was, I had to buy a christening present for my god-daughter. But, once I got into the cool, gorgeous halls of Tiffany, something *happened*. I'm at a loss to describe it really, except that there were all these *beautiful things*. Pendants and bracelets and watches and earrings and little silver hand-mirrors and cute chunky keyrings. Suddenly it made perfect sense to buy presents for everyone I knew for the rest of their lives. I decided to buy my sister a silver wedding anniversary present. Even though she's not actually married. Or engaged. Or going out with someone. Then I wanted to buy my son a watch for his twenty-first, and it didn't seem to be any impediment whatso*ever* that I don't have children.

Eventually I got away with the christening present, a 'piece' for my sister's Christmas present (it was April) and a present for Himself's birthday, five months hence. And then the wrapping began – an intricate and deeply soothing process, like watching delicate, skilled hands produce the finest origami. First they put the item in a little black velvet box, then in a duck-egg blue suede pouch, then in a matching Tiffany box, tied up with a white satin Tiffany ribbon and finally in a Tiffany bag. I've never seen such beautiful wrapping. I felt so over-come it was a bit like the part in *The Great Gatsby* when Daisy weeps, 'I've never seen such beautiful shirts.'

Out in the street, it was like waking up from the most pleasant dream. Except that I had all these duck-egg blue carrier bags and a great dread of receiving my next credit card bill.

Villa-itis

Villa-itis. *n*. The fear, while trapped with your entire family in a villa just outside Cannes, of running out of bread.

It started even before we left. About a week before the off, my mother rang me and she sounded anxious. 'You know when we're in that house in the South of France? Shouldn't we organise some sort of kitty?'

This baffled me because the one thing you can say about my family is that we pay our way. In fact, it can almost get ugly. There were going to be ten adults and two children in the house for the week and everyone was going to be trying their hardest not just to 'stand their round' grocerically-speaking, but to be the first to do so. I reminded Mammy Keyes of this but she refused to be mollified. 'What if I come down for my breakfast and someone's eaten all my bread and I can't make toast?'

Then I understood. She didn't mean a kitty, she meant self-determination over food. Kind of understandable: my family are all adults now, used to living on our own or with a small number of other people, whom we can monitor, hawk-eyed, to make sure they stay away from our bread. Suddenly we were going to be thrust into a situation with several other hungry people and it would be a hard job to track them all. But what was Mammy K proposing? Everyone getting a shelf in the French fridge for their own food, like in a flat-share? Even putting little notes on things? 'Tadhg's butter. It's been weighed!' Or (when in Rome) *'Les Muller Corners de Marian. Ne touchez-pas!'*

I tried to jolly her along with talk that it would all work itself out. But clearly she wasn't convinced because a rumour reached me that, along with her sundresses, sandals, suncream, etc, she was planning to bring a sliced pan in her suitcase. Allegedly (according to my source) she would keep said bread under lock and key for the week, only opening the vault once a day, to retrieve two slices to carry downstairs for her breakfast toast. She would swagger past all the hungry hordes who were too proud or too foolish to think ahead like she had, saunter into the kitchen, approach the toaster and make toast. When I confronted her, she would neither confirm nor deny it. But when I made mention of my nephew Luka's fondness for OPT (Other People's Toast – it is as ambrosia to him, rendered unbearably delicious by the fact of belonging to some-one else) and that she wouldn't be able to resist giving it to him, because no one can refuse him anything ever, I could see her doing mental calculations, to see if she had enough slices to bring down an extra one each day for Luka. Evidently the sums added up because her brow cleared and the serene 'I've got my own bread' expres-sion resumed residence on her face.

Anyway, on a Saturday in early September, twelve of us descended on a beautiful house just outside Cannes. We came from all three corners of the globe – Prague, where my brother lives with his wife Ljiljana and their two children, New York, where my sister Caitríona lives and Dublin where the rest of us reside.

We got through the first night's dinner without any mention of bread because the caretaker had prepared us a meal so delicious that we were distracted. Then the following morning, Himself and myself saddled up to go to *le supermarché* to buy supplies for the twelve of us. Everyone had special requests – goat's cheese, drinking chocolate, Special K bars, blackcurrant Winders (that was me) – but even in these carb-phobic times, bread was the one common thread. It was what everyone wanted. It made sense: we were self-catering and as we're not the kind of family who 'rustles' things up – blanching peppers and making our own balsamic vinegar dressing and preparing a 'delicious, light lunch' in fifteen minutes – bread was vital. We could make cheese sangwidges. We could make hang sangwidges. We could make cheese *and* hang sangwidges. Sure, you wouldn't even need a plate.

Actually, it's not entirely true to say that no one in the family can rustle up delicious meals in seconds. One member is spectacularly gifted. I need hardly say she is not from the original gene-pool, but 'brought in'. I speak of my sister-in-law, Ljiljana, (The Most Fabulous Woman On The Planet™). But she was on her holidays, so why should she be producing indescribably delicious fresh

47

tomato soup from 'bits and pieces that were lying around in the fridge'. Also Himself's admiration for Ljiljana is very, very high. I wasn't keen for her to do anything to fan the flames.

Leaving for le supermarché, I was badly jostled by the front door as everyone insisted on giving me money to pay for le shopping. ('*I'll* get it.' 'No, *I'll* get it.' 'Je . . . moi . . . le . . . ah feck it, I'll get it.') Festooned with bank-notes like an Afghani bride, I left. (Is it Afghani I'm thinking of? Maybe it's Uzbek? Or Armenian?) Just before the car turned out on to the road an upstairs window opened and a disembodied voice called, 'Get some bread!'

We bought four loaves, which seemed like enough for one day – after all, we would be going to le supermarché or even le boulangerie *chaque jour*. Then we came home and a lovely, casual day unfolded. People sunbathed, swam, shoved each other off lilos and wandered in and out of the kitchen for their lunch sangwidges whenever they felt like it. (Me? I usually like my lunch around 10.45.)

But some time in the early afternoon, Dad rushed out of the kitchen, stood at the top of the steps that descended to the garden and, like a general returning with news of an unexpected and dreadful defeat in battle, wailed at the prone bodies by the pool, 'All the bread is gone!'

I was mortified! It had been my responsibility to buy enough bread and I hadn't. Dad assembled a pitiful repast of Special K bars, goat's cheese and blackcurrant

Winders and although he made the best of it, he was obviously upset.

(But later, in the admittedly large kitchen, I stumbled across an almost full baguette hidden beneath a tea-towel. Further investigation revealed another loaf – hello? – in the bread-bin. And half a brioche on the draining board.)

But the damage – or *damage* – had been done. We were all in the grip of a hysteria, a terror of running out.

The following day more people went on the official trip to le supermarché and bought *five* loaves. Then Niall and Tadhg arrived home from golf bearing several eight-foot-long baguettes. Five minutes later Dad appeared – he'd been missing all morning – apparently he'd walked the three kilometres into the centre of Cannes and he too was laden with bread.

We had far too much, but it still wasn't enough. It was like we had become blind to what was really there and acquisition was the only thing that was important. (Some kind of metaphor about life there, if I could only be arsed to pursue it.)

The following day, the situation reached its high water mark. I wasn't there (in the spa in Hotel Martinez, another story) but apparently Dad did a reprise of his general-returning-with-news-of-defeat act. There was NO BREAD!

Ljiljana, demonstrating she is more than worthy of her title (The Most Fabulous Woman On The Planet™) offered to *bake* bread. For some reason she happened to have a packet of bread-mix about her person. And I returned, reeking of lavender oil, to the bizarre sight of Ljiljana, in a kitchen that seemed to be heaving with bread, *baking bread*.

I have since discovered that it's not just that my family are insane, although of course they are, but that this fear of running out is a 'Villa thing'. A syndrome that has something to do with displacement and temporary lack of domestic autonomy. My friend Shoshana went to a villa in Spain with her family and experienced an almost identical situation with bread. People were actually hoarding the stuff, she said, even though they had so much bread they had run out of cupboard space and had taken to stacking it on the floor. Then one day she and her mother went on a trip to Gibraltar and discovered the local branch of Marks and Spencer. Despite being surrounded by Marks and Spencers at home, they got very excited. (This is a holiday feature for me, too – shops that I can visit any time I like at home, suddenly seem like Aladdin's Caves of wondrousness.) What could be nicer, they thought, than to buy Marks and Spencer sandwiches for everyone? All of a doodah they hurried home and exclaimed, 'M&S sangers all round!' The others stretched to see over the uneaten columns of bread and gave grateful thanks that now there was something to eat for lunch.

Eyes Wide Shut

A few years ago a plethora of Keyes' went to visit Niall and Co. in Prague for Christmas, hoping for snow, hand-made wooden toys and a merciful break from turkey. (Carp is their thing, apparently.) Unfortunately there wasn't room for everyone to stay in Niall's apartment (all mittel-European charm and atmosphere, with lovely, funny windows and strange names like Skvorecky and Havranova on the doorbell.) Never mind, we sez, a hotel will do – only to discover that an alarming number of Prague hotels were closed over Christmas.

Eventually, and in a bit of a panic, we found a place – Hotel Praha – on the internet. They claimed they'd be happy to take us. Strangely, it wasn't in any guide books and, although it was a mere five minutes walk from Niall's apartment, he'd never heard of it. God only knew what it was like, but what choice did we have?

I'll admit it: from the off, the omens weren't good. First the flight from Dublin to London was massively delayed and we were terrified we'd miss our connection. The moment we landed in London, we had to do an undignified, sweaty, inter-terminal trolley dash, with some of the older and more infirm members of our party crouched amongst the bags, holding on to the trolley edges for dear life. In the nick of time, the *nick of time* – that's what they kept telling us – we made the flight, the door slamming behind us the minute we wheezed aboard – and then! We went nowhere! We sat for what felt like days on the runway – at the very point at which it dawned on us how terribly, slaveringly hungry we were. We hadn't eaten all day and wouldn't be getting anything until the plane took off, if it ever did and if it hadn't been for my mother's emergency stash of peanut M&Ms, we'd have started eating each other, like in that film about the plane crash in the Andes.

Worse was to come. When we landed in Prague, my bag with all my Christmas presents in it hadn't made the journey. (I have extremely bad luggage karma. In a past life I must have been a baggage handler who nicked loads of stuff out of unlocked suitcases.) I'm so used to losing bags at this stage that I don't bother waiting at the luggage carousel any more; I go straight to the lost luggage desk and start filling out the forms.

The rest of my family, complete with their luggage – lucky bastards – went on ahead, and when I'd filled in enough missing-bag documents to satisfy Czech bureaucracy, myself and Himself finally arrived at Hotel Praha. Now, at this point, it's important to remember I've had a long stressful day, all I've had to eat is seven peanut M&Ms and my bag with all my lovingly purchased presents has disappeared and I'm fully convinced I'll never see them again.

'Welcome to Hotel Praha!' the super-cheery deskman said. 'You are very late. Very, very late. So we have put you in a special room!' Naturally enough, the day having gone so badly, I presumed he meant a six-foot square windowless box and I prepared to vault over the counter to savage him. But I paused mid-crouch when he continued, 'When Tom Cruise was making *Mission Impossible* in Prague he stayed in the same suite for six weeks! Nicole cooked him dinner there!'

I narrowed my eyes at him. Taking the piss, was he? But what if . . . could there be a chance that maybe . . . he wasn't? Cautiously I accepted my key, gave him an I'll-be-back-if-I-need-to look and made for our 'special room'.

And your man wasn't joking. Our room was very special – it was *enormous*, far bigger than our house in Dublin. It took ten minutes to walk from one end of the sitting room to the other (I'm exaggerating only slightly), it had four bathrooms, a dining table that seated twelve, an office and a massive balcony which overlooked Prague Castle. (All the rooms have the same view.) And so what if I occasionally got an electric shock when I touched anything metal, and did it matter that the bathroom doors were constructed in such a way that if you closed the door while still holding the handle (and how else are you to do it?) your fingers become painfully trapped?

It was costing us eighty dollars a night. Forty dollars each. For. Nothing. My parents and siblings came to ooh and aah and I swaggered about, delighted with the sudden change in my fortunes.

'Now aren't you glad your bag got lost?' Mam asked. 'Come on, we've to go down for our carp. Listen, are they telling the truth about Tom Cruise?'

Hard to know, but over the next few days enough staff swore blind that Tom really did stay in that self-same room, and that Nicole really did visit him there, to convince me. As it happened, one of my Christmas presents was a velvet eye-mask (to aid restful sleep on bright summer mornings) but it came in very handy as a prop as Himself and myself pretended to be Tom and Nicole in *Eyes Wide Shut*. Oh, *hours* of fun.

In the daylight we got a better look at the hotel and it was *gas*. Finished in 1981, it was the Czech attempt at late-seventies-luxe. They were showing off – look at our most excellent, Vestern-style hotel, see how well the Soviet system is vorking for us hard-vorking Czech – and many of the big names stayed there: Brezhnev, Andropov, Ceauşescu.

No expense was spared in its interior: every single wall and door is clad in walnut and the scale of the place is *massive*. There's a swimming pool, tennis courts, a beauty salon and expansive gardens. Even a skitless (sic) alley. (Badly crap, mind you.) The outside is text-book Czech modernist architecture – mucho, mucho concrete, but it is curved and graceful; from the air it would look like a giant 'S' shape.

And it wasn't just the architecture that was central European, and timewarped: the room service menu listed ten different breakfasts, as follows. (I *love* this.) Breakfast # 1: 50g of domestic cheese and 50g of cold meat. Breakfast # 2: 100g of domestic cheese. Breakfast # 3: 100g of cold meats. And so on. Such precision dates from Soviet times when the fear of being swizzed was high. You could bring your own personal weighing scales just to check that the room-service boy hadn't helped himself to a 5g corner of your cheese en route from the kitchen. (Of course you pay a premium for having your 100g of cheese delivered to your room – a whopping 2 euro will be added to your bill.) However, the charming staff are not Soviet-style and are more than prepared to go 'off-menu.' I've requested – and been given – a non-menu yoghurt. And another time, a fruit salad. And another time, a banana.

However, the 'orange' 'juice' is authentically terrifying. It's a long way from an orange that their 'orange' 'juice' was reared: syrup-thick and day-glo, like undiluted Miwadi. And the mini-bar is charmingly bereft of produce – a couple of bottles of local beer and some dodgy-looking, chemical-filled soft drinks is all you'll get.

On account of Ema and Luka, Himself and myself go to Prague a lot and we always stay at the Praha – although sadly we never got the Tom Cruise suite again, but even the ordinary rooms have character and space.

For ages, we seemed to be the only people there. Although there are four floors, we were only ever put on the first, leading us to suspect that the other three floors were covered in dust-sheets, like a hotel version of Miss Havisham, waiting for the visitors to return. And then, lo and behold, they did! On a recent visit the Germans had arrived, busloads of them. Filming something. A fashion show, perhaps. Or . . . or . . . maybe a porn film. Lots of busty blonde women running around in see-through tops and beardy men in leather trousers filming them.

Then, another time we went – how bizarre is this? – and the Galway Choral Society were doing a concert. Luka and Ema were wheeled along to experience the Irish side of their heritage and Luka was evidently very moved because, during a sixteen-part harmony of 'Danny Boy', he lunged at the front row of warblers with his plastic knight's sword we'd bought for him in IKEA (Yes, they have IKEA in Prague) and had to be hauled off.

I love the Praha. It's a kind of memorial to a Soviet past and the staff are welcoming and incredibly obliging and, without wishing to slag the Czechs, that's not always the case. (Sometimes in Prague I'm in terrible danger of becoming the irritating kind of person who says, 'Cheer up love, it might never happen'.) It's also far enough from the town centre so if you don't want stag parties gawking their guts up outside your room every night, the Praha's your man.

Okay, it's not in the middle of town and if you need to be in staggering distance of your hotel, it's not for you. But if you're not afraid of a tram ride and you'd like to see a little remainder of Prague's recent past, you might give it a whirl. Honest to God, they're so nice. Tell them I sent you.

POCKET PENGUINS

1. Lady Chatterley's Trial
2. **Eric Schlosser** Cogs in the Great Machine
3. **Nick Hornby** Otherwise Pandemonium
4. **Albert Camus** Summer in Algiers
5. **P. D. James** Innocent House
6. **Richard Dawkins** The View from Mount Improbable
7. **India Knight** On Shopping
8. **Marian Keyes** Nothing Bad Ever Happens in Tiffany's
9. **Jorge Luis Borges** The Mirror of Ink
10. **Roald Dahl** A Taste of the Unexpected
11. **Jonathan Safran Foer** The Unabridged Pocketbook of Lightning
12. **Homer** The Cave of the Cyclops
13. **Paul Theroux** Two Stars
14. **Elizabeth David** Of Pageants and Picnics
15. **Anaïs Nin** Artists and Models
16. **Antony Beevor** Christmas at Stalingrad
17. **Gustave Flaubert** The Desert and the Dancing Girls
18. **Anne Frank** The Secret Annexe
19. **James Kelman** Where I Was
20. **Hari Kunzru** Noise
21. **Simon Schama** The Bastille Falls
22. **William Trevor** The Dressmaker's Child
23. **George Orwell** In Defence of English Cooking
24. **Michael Moore** Idiot Nation
25. **Helen Dunmore** Rose, 1944
26. **J. K. Galbraith** The Economics of Innocent Fraud
27. **Gervase Phinn** The School Inspector Calls
28. **W. G. Sebald** Young Austerlitz
29. **Redmond O'Hanlon** Borneo and the Poet
30. **Ali Smith** Ali Smith's Supersonic 70s
31. **Sigmund Freud** Forgetting Things
32. **Simon Armitage** King Arthur in the East Riding
33. **Hunter S. Thompson** Happy Birthday, Jack Nicholson
34. **Vladimir Nabokov** Cloud, Castle, Lake
35. **Niall Ferguson** 1914: Why the World Went to War

POCKET PENGUINS